IT'S TIME TO LEARN ABOUT COWBIRDS

It's Time to Learn about Cowbirds

Walter the Educator

Silent King Books
A WhichHead Entertainment Imprint

Copyright © 2025 by Walter the Educator

All rights reserved. No part of this book may be reproduced in any manner whatsoever without written per- mission except in the case of brief quotations embodied in critical articles and reviews.

First Printing, 2024

Disclaimer

This book is a literary work; the story is not about specific persons, locations, situations, and/or circumstances unless mentioned in a historical context. Any resemblance to real persons, locations, situations, and/or circumstances is coincidental. This book is for entertainment and informational purposes only. The author and publisher offer this information without warranties expressed or implied. No matter the grounds, neither the author nor the publisher will be accountable for any losses, injuries, or other damages caused by the reader's use of this book. The use of this book acknowledges an understanding and acceptance of this disclaimer.

It's Time to Learn about Cowbirds is a collectible early learning book by Walter the Educator suitable for all ages belonging to Walter the Educator's Time to Eat Book Series. Collect more books at WaltertheEducator.com

USE THE EXTRA SPACE TO TAKE NOTES AND DOCUMENT YOUR MEMORIES

COWBIRDS

The cowbird's feathers are dark and sleek,

It's Time to Learn about
Cowbirds

With glossy black and a curious beak.

You might not hear them moo or low,

But "cow" is still the name they know!

Why the name? Well, here's the clue

They followed cows their whole life through.

They'd eat the bugs kicked up by hooves,

In grassy fields where cattle moves.

The cowbird is a clever guest,

But doesn't build its own soft nest.

Instead, it lays eggs on the sly

In nests of birds that flutter by.

This trick is called "brood parasitism,"

A big word, yes, but not a prison!

It means they leave their chicks to grow

In someone else's nest below.

It's Time to Learn about
Cowbirds

The other birds will raise the chick,

And feed it worms so it grows quick.

Though not their own, they still take care,

As if their eggs were always there.

Cowbird chicks grow fast and wide,

Sometimes they take up all the side!

The other chicks might get less food,

Which isn't always kind or good.

Still, cowbirds learned this long ago,

To help their baby numbers grow.

It may seem strange, but in the wild,

There's many ways to raise a child.

They don't stay long in one set place,

They travel far with steady pace.

So building nests would slow them down

It's Time to Learn about
Cowbirds

They'd miss the fields and miss the town!

So next time that you take a look

At bird nests near a stream or brook,

You might just see a baby there

That's not like others, big and rare!

Now you know the cowbird's way

A traveling bird that doesn't stay.

It's part of nature's clever plan,

It's Time to Learn about
Cowbirds

One more surprise in birdland's span!

ABOUT THE CREATOR

Walter the Educator is one of the pseudonyms for Walter Anderson. Formally educated in Chemistry, Business, and Education, he is an educator, an author, a diverse entrepreneur, and he is the son of a disabled war veteran. "Walter the Educator" shares his time between educating and creating. He holds interests and owns several creative projects that entertain, enlighten, enhance, and educate, hoping to inspire and motivate you. Follow, find new works, and stay up to date with Walter the Educator™

at WaltertheEducator.com

www.ingramcontent.com/pod-product-compliance
Lightning Source LLC
LaVergne TN
LVHW051920060526
838201LV00060B/4098